The National Park Service takes care of wild areas.

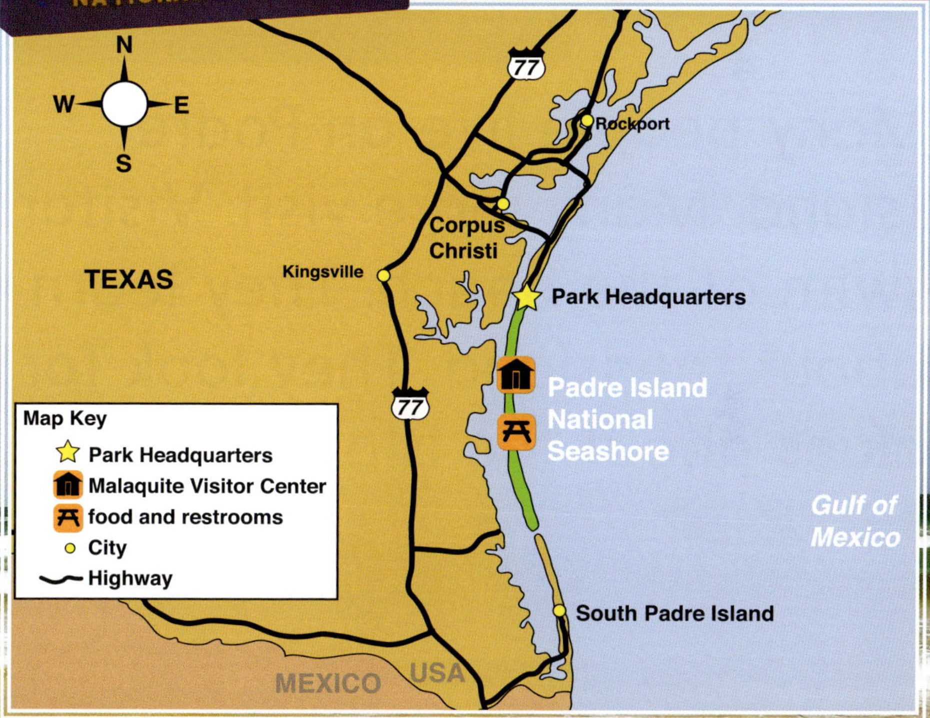

Map Key
- ★ Park Headquarters
- 🏠 Malaquite Visitor Center
- 🎋 food and restrooms
- • City
- — Highway

Chapter 1:

Visiting the National Park

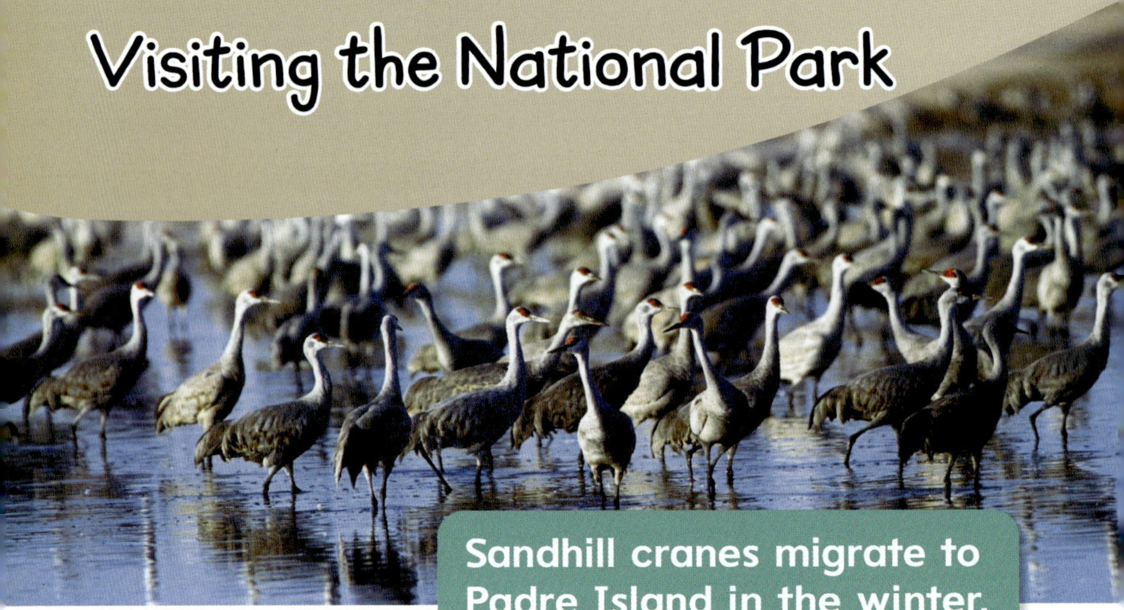

Sandhill cranes migrate to Padre Island in the winter.

Many people live on Padre Island. Many more visit. Visitors swim at the beach. They learn about the island. They look for **clues** about the island's history.

Fishing is a popular activity on Padre Island.

(t) U.S. National Park Service (NPS), (b) philipus/Alamy Stock Photo

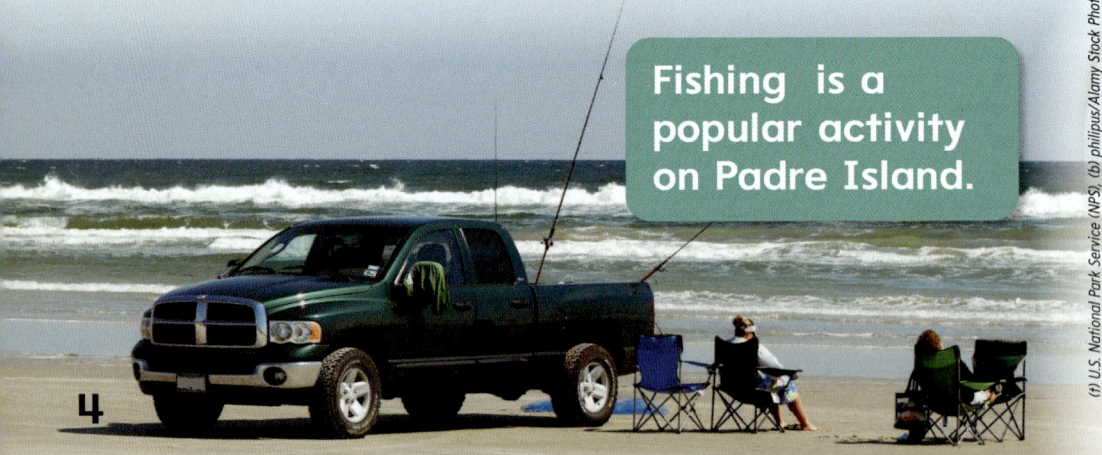

Introduction

Padre Island **National** Seashore is on an island off the coast of Texas. It is **protected** by the National Park Service. The National Park Service takes care of parks and **monuments**. It makes rules to protect plants and animals.

Genre Argumentative Text

Essential Question
How do landmarks help us understand our country's story?

Preserving a Special Place
by Susan Sklar

Introduction 2

Chapter 1
Visiting the National Park 4

Chapter 2
Dangers to Wildlife 8

Chapter 3
Finding Solutions 12

Conclusion 14

Respond to Reading 15

PAIRED READ Gateway Arch 16

Focus on Social Studies 19

Visitors use boats to **explore**. They go fishing and camp on the beach.

There are many kinds of birds in the park. People visit the park to see them. A **massive** number of birds migrate to the park.

Why Do Birds Migrate?

Many birds migrate, or move from one place to another. They fly south in winter to find warmth, food, and safe places to nest. They return north in the summer.

Padre Island National Seashore is getting more visitors. More restaurants and stores are opening. People are building **grand** hotels.

The city of Corpus Christi attracts visitors to the island.

Rules protect the park's wildlife. Humans can hurt the park. Cars and trash hurt animals. Wind and waves have **carved** sand hills on the beaches. Visitors **damage** these dunes.

STOP AND CHECK

How can visitors harm the park?

Park rangers collect trash that pollutes the island.

Chapter 2:
Dangers to Wildlife

Baby sea turtles crawl to the ocean.

Kemp's ridley sea turtles live on the island. Females come to lay eggs. Baby turtles crawl to the ocean after they **hatch**.

The sea turtles are endangered. This means they can **disappear** forever. Human activity harms them. Rangers move nests to safe places.

Rangers count eggs to track the turtle population.

Park rangers help baby turtles to safety.

Some birds on Padre Island are in danger. Birds have **fewer** places to nest. People and loud noises scare birds away.

What Does a Park Ranger Do?

Park rangers protect nature and educate park guests. Rangers learn about animals and plants. Some rangers work for a short time in different parks.

Birds' Nests on Padre Island

Many people want to protect the animals. They want visitors to stay away from nests.

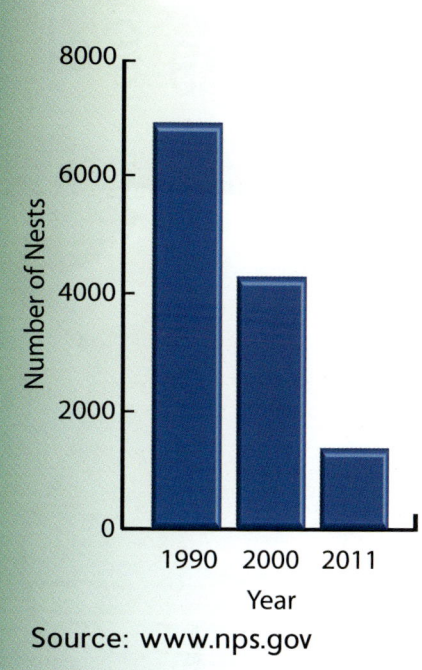

Source: www.nps.gov

This graph shows the decrease in the number of nests.

STOP AND CHECK

How can people protect the island's birds?

Chapter 3: Finding Solutions

Rules protect birds such as these spoonbills.

People want to protect Padre Island National Seashore. Others don't want too many rules. Is there a solution?

Visitors can watch the animals. But they cannot feed them.

Cars are only allowed in some areas.

Cars must drive slowly on the beach. They are not allowed to drive where plants grow or animals nest.

Visitors can bring food to the beach. They can leave no **traces** of their visit. Visitors must leave the beach as they found it.

STOP AND CHECK

Why does the National Park Service have rules for visitors?

Conclusion

Humans can harm the Padre Island National Seashore. But some simple rules can protect it. And people can still enjoy the park. This famous **landmark** is a special place.

Respond to Reading

Summarize

Summarize what you have learned about Padre Island National Seashore. Use details from the text. Your chart may help you.

Main Idea
The National Park Service is finding solutions to protect wildlife in the park.
Detail
Detail
Detail

Text Evidence

1. Why is Padre National Seashore important? **MAIN IDEA AND DETAILS**

2. Find the word *protected* on page 2. What does it mean? What clues help you figure it out? **VOCABULARY**

3. Write about some of the animals of Padre Island. **WRITE ABOUT READING**

Genre Expository Text

Compare Texts
Read about the tallest monument in the United States.

GATEWAY ARCH

Gateway Arch is in St. Louis. It is the tallest monument in the United States. It honors explorers who settled the West.

Many people began their journey west from St. Louis.

16

Luther Ely Smith planned the grand monument.

A contest was held. The best design was chosen. Eero Saarinen won. Building began in 1963. The arch opened in 1967.

Explorers William Clark (left) and Meriwether Lewis (right) began their journey west in St. Louis.

The Gateway Arch is 630 feet tall. Visitors can ride to the top. They can see all of St. Louis.

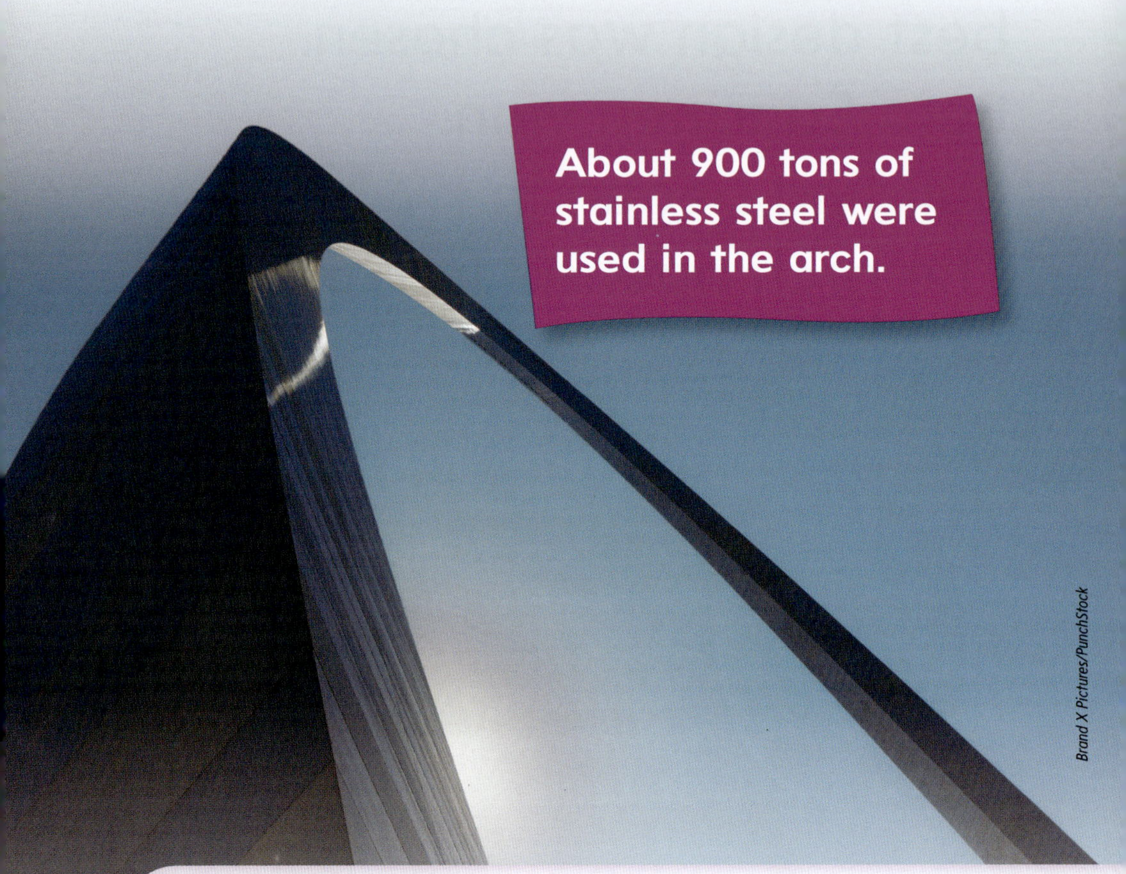

About 900 tons of stainless steel were used in the arch.

Make Connections

What does Gateway Arch honor?
ESSENTIAL QUESTION

How is Gateway Arch like Padre Island National Seashore?
TEXT TO TEXT

Focus on Social Studies

Purpose To learn about a landmark in your state

What to do

Step 1 With a partner, make a poster about a landmark in your state. Draw a picture and a map of where it is located.

Step 2 List five facts about this landmark. How big is it? When was it built? Who built it? How many people visit every year?

Step 3 Talk about the landmark with your partner.

Step 4 Share what you learned with the class.

Conclusion Why are landmarks important?